KITTY STEALS A DOG

A one-act comedy by
Keegon Schuett

www.youthplays.com
info@youthplays.com
424-703-5315

 ISBN 978-1-62088-184-2.

COPYRIGHT RULES TO REMEMBER

1. To produce this play, you must receive prior written permission from YouthPLAYS and pay the required royalty.

2. You must pay a royalty each time the play is performed in the presence of audience members outside of the cast and crew. Royalties are due whether or not admission is charged, whether or not the play is presented for profit, for charity or for educational purposes, or whether or not anyone associated with the production is being paid.

3. No changes, including cuts or additions, are permitted to the script without written prior permission from YouthPLAYS.

4. Do not copy this book or any part of it without written permission from YouthPLAYS.

5. Credit to the author and YouthPLAYS are required on all programs and other promotional items associated with this play's performance.

When you pay royalties, you are recognizing the hard work that went into creating the play and making a statement that a play is something of value. We think this is important, and we hope that everyone will do the right thing, thus allowing playwrights to generate income and continue to create wonderful new works for the stage.

Plays are owned by the playwrights who wrote them. Violating a playwright's copyright is a very serious matter and violates both United States and international copyright law. Infringement is punishable by actual damages and attorneys' fees, statutory damages of up to $150,000 per incident, and even possible criminal sanctions. **Infringement is theft. Don't do it.**

Have a question about copyright? Please contact us by email at info@youthplays.com or by phone at 424-703-5315. When in doubt, please ask.

CAST OF CHARACTERS

KITTY, an unwilling ballerina; bold, daring; maybe too intimidating.

LIAM, nervous perfectionist and wallflower; secretly witty.

REBECCA, popular, but not heartless. Very pretty.

CHARLIE, the one guy everyone loves to hate.

PRODUCTION NOTE

It is possible to substitute "butts" for "asses" depending on the standards of your community.

SCENE 1

(A residential fence. A teenage boy standing behind a lemonade stand. It's a little too put together for its own good. He is also a little too put together for his own good. He is LIAM. A girl dressed in a pink tutu and ballet slippers stands nearby. She has a satchel over one shoulder. It's decorated with delightfully witty buttons. This is KITTY. She and Liam are fighting over a stack of flyers. She is hitting him with a roll of tape.)

KITTY: Hey, stop it!

LIAM: I told you not to put them on my stand.

KITTY: Quit it.

LIAM: You weren't listening to me. I'm making a stand.

KITTY: Oh, you're making a stand about your lemonade stand? Cute.

LIAM: You weren't listening to me so—

(He tears another flyer in half. She throws down her satchel.)

KITTY: Give them back.

LIAM: No!

KITTY: Give them back now!

LIAM: You shouldn't have taped them to my stand.

KITTY: I asked if I could.

LIAM: Did not.

KITTY: Did too.

LIAM: Liar.

KITTY: You're the liar.

LIAM: Sour apple.

KITTY: Sour...lemon!

(He tears another flyer in half.)

Fine, you know what—

LIAM: What?!

KITTY: You know what?

LIAM: What?

KITTY: I don't know what! *(Beat.)* But I'm taking your stupid cashbox for emotional compensation. And I'll print more flyers. So there!

(She grabs his cashbox and begins to walk away. Liam grabs her arm.)

LIAM: No, wait!

KITTY: Let go of my arm!

LIAM: I'll give back your flyers.

KITTY: Why?

LIAM: I'm sorry. So I'll give them back.

KITTY: Is there a lot of money in here?

LIAM: No, I just—

KITTY: Wow. There's a lot of money in here.

LIAM: No. Just give it back!

KITTY: Too late!

(She starts to run around the lemonade stand with the cashbox. Liam chases her.)

LIAM: Don't make me run! When I get you I'm gonna—

KITTY: What?! You can't hit me. I'm a girl.

LIAM: You're a ballerina.

KITTY: I am not a ballerina. *(Beat.)* Are you saying it's okay to hit ballerinas?

LIAM: You're dressed like one.

KITTY: Well, you're dressed like an idiot.

LIAM: I'm dressed like a businessman.

(He catches the cashbox; they struggle over it, pulling it back and forth between the two of them. They fall backwards, dropping the cashbox and it spills coins all over the ground. Kitty and Liam are silent. Kitty laughs.)

KITTY: Vast riches you've got there, Mr. Lemonade Tycoon.

LIAM: Don't make fun of me.

KITTY: I'm not. I'm—I'm sorry. I was being a bit—

LIAM: You're a bully.

KITTY: How did you know?

LIAM: Know what?

KITTY: Girls in my ballet class. They call me the Bully Ballerina. One of my many nicknames.

LIAM: Sorry.

KITTY: Don't be. *(Beat.)* I'm sorry. I'll help you clean up.

LIAM: Okay.

(They start putting the coins back in the cashbox.)

I don't even have any nicknames.

KITTY: How come?

LIAM: I don't hang out with people. I don't want to either.

KITTY: Ooh, they should call you: The Loner.

LIAM: I've been invited before, of course.

KITTY: Totally, of course. Me too.

LIAM: But I don't go. Because I don't want to go to Starbucks.

KITTY: Me either. *(Beat.)* I don't remember your name.

LIAM: I never told you. We're casual acquaintances.

KITTY: More like business casual.

LIAM: What?

KITTY: Your suit. That was a joke.

LIAM: Oh. Ha ha.

(He extends his hand.)

I'm Liam.

(She extends her hand.)

KITTY: It's Katherine. But people call me Kitty. Another nickname.

(They shake hands for the next few lines of dialogue.)

LIAM: I actually knew that.

KITTY: Yeah, it's unfortunate how nicknames work. When they stick—

LIAM: They're stuck.

KITTY: Can't unstick them.

LIAM: Unstickable.

KITTY: Yep. Can I have my hand back now?

LIAM: Oh! Sorry.

(He lets go.)

You know what...I will post a flyer on my stand.

KITTY: You will? That's allowed?

LIAM: Yeah, it is a good cause.

(She hands him a flyer. He looks at it.)

When'd she go missing?

KITTY: *He* went missing about a week and a half ago.

LIAM: What's his name?

KITTY: Spot.

LIAM: But he doesn't have spots.

KITTY: I'm not particularly creative in the name department.

(A moment. Then terror:)

LIAM: Oh, no.

KITTY: What?

LIAM: Rebecca Pierce.

KITTY: From school?

LIAM: Yes.

KITTY: So?

LIAM: So she's coming this way.

KITTY: What? Do you have a crush on her or something?

LIAM: No!

KITTY: Aw, c'mon, you can tell me.

LIAM: She's coming over here. *(Beat.)* Hide.

KITTY: Hide?

LIAM: Yes.

KITTY: Now?

LIAM: Hide!

KITTY: Okay, okay!

(She darts under his lemonade stand. She pops her head up:)

Why am I hiding?

LIAM: I'll explain later, but just hide now quick. Please thank you.

(He pushes her head down. Then he attempts to strike a charismatic and relaxed pose and fails on both counts. REBECCA enters.)

Hey. Hi. Hey. How's it going, Rebecca?

REBECCA: It's going okay. What're you doing?

LIAM: Oh, you know, not much just chilling. Just chillaxing. Chilling and relaxing. Hanging out. Chilling. You? What're you doing?

REBECCA: I was just going for a walk.

LIAM: Yeah? A walk? I like walking. I do it a lot actually. Ha ha. Where were you walking?

REBECCA: Just around the neighborhood. *(Beat.)* Are you selling lemonade?

LIAM: I—me? I'm—no. No.

REBECCA: It looks like you're selling lemonade.

LIAM: No, not me. I mean, yes. Yes, I'm helping my...cousin. She's five. Lemonade's cool for her. I think it's lame unless you think it's cool. Then we could chill. Chillax with some lemonade.

REBECCA: No, sorry. I'd like to, but I can't.

(She makes to leave.)

LIAM: Yeah, I understand. Cool, well, cool. Nice talking to you. Seeing you.

REBECCA: Yeah, you too. *(Sees the flyer:)* Aw, what a cute dog.

LIAM: Yeah. Yeah! It's a cute dog. Very missing. Cute, cuddly dog. Do you like dogs?

REBECCA: Yeah. I've got two.

LIAM: I like dogs too. I bet I'd like your two dogs too. Ha ha. Two, too. Tutu.

REBECCA: Ha ha. *(Beat.)* Well, I'm headed home. Talk to you later, Adam.

LIAM: Yeah, see ya, Rebecca.

(She exits. Liam deflates a bit. Kitty rises from behind the lemonade stand. She pours him a glass of lemonade. She slides it toward him.)

KITTY: Looks like you could use this. *(Beat.)* It's on the house.

(He takes it and chugs the lemonade. He sits in front of the stand. Kitty walks around and sits next to him.)

That was rough, man.

LIAM: No, I think that definitely went well.

KITTY: I'm fluent in sarcasm so... *(Beat.)* I mean, I get it.

LIAM: Every time I see her... I mean, I plan out conversations. Entire conversations. "Hi, Rebecca. You look lovely today." *(Beat.)* "Thank you, Liam. How kind of you to say. You're looking sharp yourself." Etcetera etcetera. I mean, do you do that? Does anyone else do this?

KITTY: No. But I used to have lengthy conversations with my dog. Mostly about his day.

LIAM: I really hope you find him. Man's best friend.

KITTY: *My* best friend.

LIAM: You know, I don't even have a best friend.

KITTY: Everyone has a best friend.

LIAM: Not me.

(Silence.)

KITTY: Okay, maybe this is weird... I don't know, maybe not. But. I have a proposition.

LIAM: Uh-huh.

KITTY: I don't have any friends and you don't have any friends. Neither of us have human friends. My dog is missing and you want to get to second base with Rebecca.

LIAM: Second base?

KITTY: It's baseball. Make out. Making out.

LIAM: Oh, but I—

KITTY: It's fine. You don't need to be ashamed of it. It's fairly obvious. *(Beat.)* So here's what it is...how about this: we help each other out. I help you get your girlfriend. You help me find my dog. No pressure. Like a friendship.

LIAM: A friendship.

KITTY: Yeah, that's what they're called. So what do you say?

LIAM: I say sure.

KITTY: Sure.

LIAM: Sure. Let's do it.

(Silence.)

How do we—uh, start?

KITTY: One second.

(She stands and begins to walk off. Yelling:)

Hey, kid! Hey, yeah, you! No, don't run... I'm not going to hurt you, geez.

(She's gone. She returns shortly with chalk.)

The Bully Ballerina strikes again. Hope blue's okay.

(She walks to the fence and begins to write on it.)

LIAM: I don't think you should—

(She raises her free hand to silence him. She finishes and turns to him. Written on the fence is THE PLAN.)

KITTY: Okay.

LIAM: So what's the plan?

KITTY: What do we know about Rebecca Pierce?

LIAM: She's in the same grade as us.

KITTY: Alright.

(She writes their grade on the fence.)

LIAM: She lives next door.

KITTY: Good point.

(She writes GIRL NEXT DOOR on fence.)

LIAM: She's pretty.

KITTY: That's irrelevant to the situation. Were you even listening to her earlier or were you just internally drooling over her? Just because a girl's boobs start to come in doesn't mean that—

LIAM: I was listening!

KITTY: Okay! So what did she say?

LIAM: What are you asking? Like what she actually said or the underlying subtext of what she said?

KITTY: What she said and the relevant subtext, Liam.

LIAM: She was walking.

KITTY: Uh huh.

LIAM: She didn't want to hang out with me.

KITTY: Yes.

LIAM: "Cute dog." She has two dogs. She said she'd talk to me later, but that was her being nice more than her being honest probably.

KITTY: Okay! Okay! I think we can make this work. But you gotta trust me on this, okay?

LIAM: Okay. Okay, I trust you. Sort of.

KITTY: This requires absolute trust. What I'm about to say is shocking, but you need to be on board 500 percent. Or it won't work. You got it?

LIAM: Okay. You have 100 percent of my trust. 500 percent isn't really mathematically possible.

KITTY: Okay, here goes. This plan entails that we'll have to do some pretending. Can you act?

LIAM: You mean lie?

KITTY: No, no, can you pretend?

LIAM: I can try.

KITTY: You can or you will?

LIAM: I will.

KITTY: We also might have to run. Or get away. Or run. Can you run?

LIAM: I can. So what is this big plan of yours?

KITTY: Well, she's got two dogs. What do we know about that?

LIAM: She likes her dogs.

KITTY: Right, because she's got two eyes and a big, beating heart. She probably loves her dogs. And if one of them went missing, right...? She'd probably do what I'm doing and really look for them, right?

LIAM: I don't like where you're going with this.

KITTY: It'll be easy, Liam. We go next door.

LIAM: No.

KITTY: You act like you've hurt your foot.

LIAM: No.

KITTY: Or something worse...like...like like—an allergic reaction. To your lemonade! You fake an allergic reaction to your lemonade.

LIAM: No. C'mon.

KITTY: I run inside to "make a phone call" to get an "ambulance." Instead, I nab the dog...whichever one is smaller... I sneak out. You get a glass of water.

LIAM: This is an awful idea.

KITTY: No, no! She realizes the dog is gone. You find the dog which makes you—

LIAM: Makes me the dog-finding hero.

KITTY: Exactly.

LIAM: Just that simple?

KITTY: That simple.

LIAM: It doesn't really sound that simple.

KITTY: It will be.

LIAM: When do we do this?

KITTY: How about now?

LIAM: Now?

KITTY: Let's roll.

(Lights out.)

SCENE 2

(In front of Rebecca's house, but almost identical to the former location. Kitty's flyers litter the fence, but there's no chalk plan or lemonade stand. Kitty and Liam enter, quickly. They're amped up and nervous.)

LIAM: We're stealing a dog.

KITTY: No. No, we're stealing a girl's heart. We're borrowing the dog to seal the deal.

LIAM: This is illegal.

KITTY: Yeah, we're breaking the "Don't Steal Dogs" law. That one.

LIAM: I don't know what it's called, but it's illegal. I'm sure.

KITTY: Calm down now. Do you want her to be your girlfriend?

LIAM: Yes. Yeah. Yes.

KITTY: Okay. Deep breaths, princess. We're doing this now.

LIAM: Okay.

KITTY: Deep breaths. Three of them and then we do this.

LIAM: Okay.

KITTY: One.

(They inhale and exhale.)

Two.

(They inhale and exhale.)

Three. *(Doesn't wait for Liam to take the breath:)* Help!

LIAM: Wait.

KITTY: No. *(Yells:)* Help! We need help over here. *(Voice down to Liam:)* Get down. Look sick. Hurry. Geez!

LIAM: I've never done this before.

KITTY: Oh, you haven't? No way! *(Firm:)* Get down. *(Yells:)* Help! I've got a sick guy over here. He could die!

(Liam is now on the ground, writhing in an entirely unconvincing manner. CHARLIE BOONE, same age as the others and a bit overweight, runs onstage.)

CHARLIE: What's wrong? I could hear you yelling from down the street.

LIAM: Oh no.

KITTY: *(Yells:)* Rebecca Pierce, help us! Charlie Boone, go away!

CHARLIE: Whoa, he doesn't look so good. I'll call 911.

KITTY: No!

LIAM: Don't!

CHARLIE: Why not? I thought you needed help.

KITTY: Charlie, you're going to ruin everything.

CHARLIE: What do you mean?

KITTY: I don't even— *(Beat.)* I can't— *(Yells:)* Rebecca, help!

CHARLIE: What is going on here?

KITTY: Nobody needs your help, Charlie.

LIAM: We've already called 911.

CHARLIE: You have?

KITTY: Yes, yeah! Of course. Are we stupid? Do we look stupid? Have you seen him? Ugh, he's sick.

LIAM: We're not stupid.

CHARLIE: Well, why are you screaming then?

KITTY: He could die! And I'm yelling, not screaming. Don't make me out to be the bad one in this situation, Charlie.

CHARLIE: I wasn't—

KITTY: God, go away, Charlie! *(Yells:)* Rebecca! Help!

CHARLIE: I'm trained in CPR if—

LIAM: No! I'll be fine.

KITTY: Go away!

CHARLIE: Fine! I was only trying to help.

(He exits.)

KITTY: That was close.

LIAM: He thought I was really sick.

KITTY: Yeah, yeah. Keep pretending. *(Yells:)* Help! Help! Help! Rebecca Pierce! Help! Help now! Help! Help! *(Beat.)* I get the feeling she doesn't want to help you.

LIAM: Here, I'll try. *(Yells:)* Help me! Help, I'm dying, I know it. Help!

KITTY: HEEEEEEELLLLLLLLPPPPPPPPPPPppppp!

(Rebecca enters. She is dressed in work-out clothes.)

REBECCA: Oh my God! Are you okay? I had my headphones in... I was—

KITTY: He's not well. He might die.

LIAM: I don't feel well. I might die.

REBECCA: Where does it hurt?

LIAM: Just...it's... I feel pain.

REBECCA: Where, Lenny?

LIAM: Liam!

REBECCA: Who's Liam? Did he do this you? Where's it hurt?

LIAM: Just...in my stomach and my...my everywhere, I guess.

KITTY: Hey! Hey! So, Rebecca...will you watch him while I go call for an ambulance?

REBECCA: Yeah. Here just use my cell phone.

(She reaches in her pocket and grabs her cell phone. She extends it to Kitty.)

KITTY: No, could I use your house phone?

REBECCA: Just use my cell phone. It's faster.

KITTY: Well, the ambulance won't be able to trace our location from your cell phone. It'll be faster to use the house phone.

REBECCA: But you're wasting time now. Just use the cell phone... Explain where we are.

KITTY: I— *(Beat.)* I...I'm afraid that cell phones give you cancer. And I don't want cancer. Where's your house phone?

REBECCA: Why are you—

KITTY: Look—we don't have time for this!

REBECCA: It's through the front door. On the left.

KITTY: Thanks!

REBECCA: Be careful... Don't let my dogs out!

KITTY: Don't worry. I won't. Don't let him die on us.

(Kitty runs off toward the door.)

REBECCA: Was she wearing a tutu?

LIAM: I think so.

REBECCA: Is she a ballerina?

LIAM: Who knows?

REBECCA: So what exactly happened, Larry?

LIAM: My name is Liam. I— *(Beat.)* The lemonade. I must be allergic.

REBECCA: You're allergic to lemonade and you were at a lemonade stand?

LIAM: I didn't know!

REBECCA: Oh. Yeah, that makes sense.

LIAM: Give me the benefit of the doubt, okay?

REBECCA: You got it. Just breathe.

LIAM: It hurts to breathe.

REBECCA: Then don't!

LIAM: I'll die.

REBECCA: Well, what can I do?

LIAM: Give me a kiss.

REBECCA: What?!

LIAM: Kiss me. That would make me feel better.

REBECCA: I'm not going to kiss you, Liam. It's Liam, right?

LIAM: You're beautiful. A kiss from a beautiful girl would help me through the— *(Painfilled noise:)* It hurts!

REBECCA: Okay, okay. But we're not going to make a habit out of it, okay?

LIAM: Just once. Just once. I won't ask ever again. I promise.

REBECCA: Okay.

(She leans in to kiss him. A large dog BARKING from inside the house, very aggressively.)

Oh, no. You don't think—I should go help.

LIAM: No, don't leave me.

REBECCA: I'm gonna go check on Kitty.

LIAM: Rebecca— I— I—

(He grabs her and kisses her. It goes on for enough time that Kitty re-enters. In her arms, a dog wrapped in a blanket...maybe only the evidence of something wrapped in a blanket. She needs to sneak past Rebecca. She makes a "Keep going" hand signal. Liam understands. He pulls Rebecca back in for a kiss. Kitty tries to sneak by. Charlie Boone reenters. He sees Kitty with the dog. Kitty runs in the opposite direction. She exits. Liam and Rebecca stop kissing.)

REBECCA: You're really good at that.

LIAM: You sound surprised.

REBECCA: I am.

LIAM: I used to practice on my hand all the time.

(Rebecca sees Charlie:)

REBECCA: Ew, Charlie!

LIAM: Charlie, were you just watching us?

REBECCA: Gross, Charlie.

CHARLIE: I wasn't—

LIAM: Shut up, Charlie. Creeping on our private moment?

REBECCA: Inappropriate.

LIAM: Perverted, really.

CHARLIE: This is a public sidewalk and that's—

REBECCA: Stop...just stop. *(To Liam:)* I'm gonna go check on Kitty. Are you feeling any better?

LIAM: Much better. Can I just have a glass of water?

REBECCA: Sure.

(She exits.)

CHARLIE: What's going on here?

LIAM: It's none of your business.

CHARLIE: You're not really sick.

LIAM: Charlie Boone. Out of my business. Please. I beg of you.

CHARLIE: What's in it for me?

LIAM: There's nothing in it for you. There's only enough for me and Kitty. It's a two-person deal.

CHARLIE: I want in.

LIAM: Of course you do, Charlie. But nobody else wants you in.

CHARLIE: I just saw Kitty steal a dog. A canine dog. I want in or I'm telling.

LIAM: Fine!

(Rebecca enters.)

REBECCA: My dog is missing.

LIAM: What about Kitty?

REBECCA: Kitty's missing too.

CHARLIE: You have a cat?

REBECCA: Go away, Charlie. *(To Liam:)* Will you help me find my dog?

CHARLIE: I'll help.

REBECCA: *(To Liam:)* Will you help me find my dog? *(To Charlie:)* Will you go away?

CHARLIE: Fine! I'm going away, but before I go... Kitty stole your dog. I said it. I'll say it again. Kitty. Stole. Your Dog. See ya, guys.

(He leaves.)

LIAM: That guy's such a jerk.

REBECCA: Is that true?

LIAM: Yeah, I don't think I've met a truer jerk in my life.

REBECCA: No, did Kitty steal my dog?

LIAM: I don't know. Do you want to look for them?

REBECCA: No, I want to find them.

(Blackout.)

SCENE 3

(The lemonade stand in front of the fence. Liam enters.)

REBECCA: *(Off:)* Max! Max!

(Liam sees the plan written on the fence. He grabs the jug of lemonade and splashes the fence with it. The chalk runs down it. Rebecca enters.)

Max! Max! Where are you, buddy? *(Beat. To Liam:)* Is he under the lemonade stand?

(Liam looks under the lemonade stand. He sees something. He stands up.)

LIAM: Nothing under there. You know what: You go on without me... I don't want to leave the stand unattended.

REBECCA: It'll be fine. Come on.

LIAM: I'm gonna count up the money, make sure no one steals it.

REBECCA: You're gonna count up four dollars' worth of quarters?

LIAM: It's important—to my cousin. She's five. I'll be right behind you...okay?

REBECCA: Okay. Fine.

(She exits. Liam waits. He hops a bit nervously in place.)

LIAM: Okay. Come out. Come out now. Wherever you are.

(Kitty emerges from beneath the stand.)

LIAM: This isn't working.

KITTY: Do you know how hard it is to run in these slippers?

LIAM: No.

KITTY: We have a problem by the way.

LIAM: I'd say we have about six. We didn't think this through.

KITTY: No, we have a real problem.

LIAM: Okay. Okay. *(Beat.)* What is it?

KITTY: I found my dog.

LIAM: That doesn't sound like a problem.

KITTY: It is. *(Beat.)* I just stole my dog from Rebecca Pierce's house.

LIAM: Wait, so—what?

KITTY: Rebecca had my dog.

LIAM: Well, you have to give it back.

KITTY: It's my dog. I don't have to give it back. The universe is back in order.

LIAM: But the plan. The plan! You're ruining the plan. I knew this would happen.

(Rebecca enters.)

REBECCA: Plan? What plan?

LIAM: There isn't a plan.

REBECCA: I just heard you. *(Beat.)* Kitty, where is my dog?

KITTY: I don't know.

REBECCA: I think you do.

LIAM: I promise you. She doesn't know.

REBECCA: I'm asking her.

KITTY: She's saying she doesn't know.

REBECCA: Where is my dog?

KITTY: I stole it. But newsflash. It is not your dog. It is my dog. My dog was missing. I found it.

REBECCA: What are you even talking about?

(Kitty pulls the flyer off of the lemonade stand.)

KITTY: Here.

(She hands it to Rebecca.)

REBECCA: So it looks like my dog.

KITTY: That's because they're the same dog. My dog.

LIAM: Ladies, if we could just—

KITTY: "Ladies?" We are not "Ladies," okay?

REBECCA: Liam, don't be such a Charlie in this situation. Please. That's the last thing we need.

KITTY: *(To Liam:)* And don't act so innocent... You helped me steal the dog after all.

REBECCA: *(To Liam:)* You did?

KITTY: Look, there's a very simple explanation to all of this.

REBECCA: Oh, I'm sure there is.

KITTY: Here goes: I lost my dog. My mom probably let him go on purpose because he poops on the carpet sometimes and I sometimes never clean it up even though I always sometimes have plenty of time to do it. I skipped ballet practice today. I post some flyers. My tutu got so sweaty and so gross. So, THEN, I meet Liam here. He likes you by the way. I'm missing my best friend. Who is a dog. So I thought, hey, let's steal her dog...whichever one's smaller...Liam returns it...you like Liam...then he helps me find my dog. Problem is...you had my dog. Spot.

REBECCA: My dog doesn't have spots.

KITTY: You're not listening. It's not your dog.

REBECCA: Max doesn't have spots.

KITTY: Yeah, well, Max isn't a dog's name.

REBECCA: Is too. Haven't you seen *The Grinch*?

LIAM: He stole Christmas.

REBECCA: He probably stole that dog too.

KITTY: Hey! Hey! Hey! My turn to talk, okay? My turn to talk!

LIAM: Fine.

REBECCA: Go.

KITTY: Look—I'm really sorry. This is all my fault. My dog is my only friend. I can't deal with handling people well. I can't even potty train my dog...or lawn train. Whatever. I think it's just best that we all go our separate ways. *(To Liam:)* You go your way. *(To Rebecca:)* You go your way. *(To herself:)* And me and Spot go our way.

REBECCA: His name is Max.

KITTY: Rebecca, I'm telling you—

REBECCA: He didn't have a collar on when I found him. Otherwise, I would've returned him...but I would really like him back.

KITTY: You've already got a dog.

LIAM: That's the wrong way to look at it.

KITTY: So now you're siding with her? *(To Rebecca:)* You have two dogs. You have that big, barking dog. Terrifying. And you've got that *(Indicates Liam:)* puppy dog. In dumb, puppy love with you. *(Beat.)* He stole a dog to get your attention.

LIAM: You stole the dog. I just helped.

KITTY: *(To Rebecca:)* Does that mean nothing to you? I mean, I'll help you find another dog. I won't steal another one. But I can go with you to the shelter if you want. Or you and Liam can go. I don't want to be a fifth wheel.

REBECCA: No. I want Max back.

KITTY: I'm sorry, but Spot isn't going with you. He's my dog.

LIAM: I really hate to get in the middle of this, but—

REBECCA: Liam, are you seriously going to side with her on this?

KITTY: Go ahead. Side with her. Her boobs are coming in really nicely so she must be right.

LIAM: I'm not going to pick sides. I'm Norway.

REBECCA: Switzerland. You're Switzerland.

KITTY: You're Liam. I actually know your name.

LIAM: Rebecca, it's not your dog. Let it go?

REBECCA: Me let it go? Me let it go? You show up on my sidewalk and act like you're dying...you steal my dog...and I'm supposed to let it go?

KITTY: It's a public sidewalk. Technically you don't own it.

REBECCA: Well, I'm not going to let this go. My dad is a lawyer. We're going to sue your asses in court. BOTH OF YOU. Your ASSES. That dog is my dog.

KITTY: Sue us for what? You stole MY dog. Did you even walk him? You must have known it was my dog...you've seen me with him. Why was MY dog in your house?

REBECCA: I don't think I like what you're trying to say. I fed the dog. I took care of the dog. MY dog.

KITTY: So you fed my dog for a week. Thanks. It's still my dog. I could sue you.

REBECCA: NO. YOU CAN'T. Both of your ASSES are sued. SUED. I will get Max back.

(She starts to exit.)

LIAM: So, can I call you?

REBECCA: NO!

(She exits.)

KITTY: Is her dad even a lawyer?

LIAM: I think so. Can she sue us?

KITTY: I have no idea. I'm sorry for dragging you into this.

LIAM: I was a willing participant. There's nothing to be sorry about. *(Beat.)* You are sure it's your dog, right?

KITTY: Pretty sure. *(Beat.)* I'm sorry about you and Rebecca.

LIAM: I don't think it was meant to be. *(Beat.)* And even if it had worked...you wouldn't have been a fifth wheel.

KITTY: Yeah?

LIAM: Technically you would have been a third wheel.

KITTY: Ha ha, yes.

LIAM: And that's not a bad thing. Lots of great things have three wheels.

KITTY: Tricycles.

LIAM: Yeah, that's one example. But there are lots of other things that—

KITTY: I think it's just tricycles. *(Beat.)* You know I don't want to be your girlfriend right?

LIAM: Yeah. I don't want to be your boyfriend.

KITTY: Oh, okay. Good.

(A moment.)

I'd still like to be friends. We wouldn't be a tricycle.

LIAM: We'd make a pretty awesome bike.

KITTY: That has two wheels.

LIAM: Yeah.

KITTY: So what do we do now?

LIAM: You want to walk your dog?

KITTY: Sure thing. *(Beat.)* This tutu is seriously killing me.

(Lights fade. The end.)

The Author Speaks

What inspired you to write this play?

Two things really inspired the writing of this play: an awkward real life experience and a character who sprang from my imagination. The real life experience stemmed from a situation in which I adopted a stray cat and then after having the cat for a month, one of my neighbors asserted that my roommate and myself had stolen her cat. She had never claimed the cat and our landlord had no idea that she claimed it, but the situation resolved itself in a very fast, weird "returning the cat" meeting. It made for interesting conversation for quite some time in our circle of friends and got me thinking about the connection people have to their pets. In addition to that, I often think graphically or visually when it comes to writing projects and there was something very intriguing about a reluctant ballerina who was very militant about finding her lost dog with stacks and stacks of homemade flyers. Once I started writing, it became clear the story was not only a mad-cap scheme about stealing a dog and stealing a girl's heart, but very fundamentally it is about the nature of modern friendship. The idea of these seemingly opposite personalities in Kitty and Liam meeting and finding that they are like-minded and well matched friends was an exciting idea to explore. I think it's important to put stories into the world that don't end with the guy getting the girl or all characters ending up perfectly coupled with one another. I wanted more literature in the world about the beauty of deliberately platonic relationships.

Was the structure of the play influenced by any other work?

Indirectly, it is. I didn't try to imitate any one particular story structure, but the zany heist structure is one that was essential to the writing of the piece. I had never written this sort of story in which everything in a straightforward plan goes awry. I find that typically I write from an emotional core of an idea instead of a situational idea, and with this piece it was actually the opposite that took place. I knew what the scheme was before I began writing...how the characters felt and reacted to it was a fun discovery I made every time I revisited it to work further.

Have you dealt with the same theme in other works that you have written?

My work, as a whole, explores the theme of self-discovery, and I think that ***Kitty Steals a Dog*** does so in a subtler way than my previous work. All characters are discovering what it truly is to interact with one another and the pitfalls of forming even casual friendships. I have dealt a lot with the idea of struggling to socialize and communicate in a modern world. This is a issue that all of the characters experience to some extent, whether it's Kitty's inability to share a meaningful relationship with someone who isn't a pet or Liam's inability to communicate with Rebecca to ask her on a date. The struggle of growing up is a very relevant one in a world in which children learn to communicate with one another via cell phones and Facebook instead of face-to-face interaction.

What writers have had the most profound effect on your style?

All writers that I encounter have a profound effect on my style and I feel that during the time when I wrote this piece, it was the first time in my life that I was more affected by the work of my peers than by "big-name" writers like Woody Allen or Edward Albee. The heavy work on this piece was completed while attending the Curious New Voices program at Curious Theatre in Denver, Colorado. It was the first time I had been consistently surrounded by people in my age group who were interested in the same things that I was interested in. This piece would not exist if I hadn't been so taken with the goofy style of Scott Egleston's writing, the madcap craziness of Mateo Correa's writing, the wit and humor of Zachary Davidson's writing. There has been no more influential month of my life as a writer on my style than I experienced in that theatre.

What do you hope to achieve with this work?
I hope to put a play into the world that people can enjoy. Life is heavy, and theatre doesn't have to be. As a person, I'm always looking for new ways to make people laugh and to bring people together and I hope that this play can be a vessel to facilitate the growth of new friendships and new appreciation for theatre. The play is meant to be quirky and it is meant to incite some discussion of modern morality and accountability, but if audiences laugh, I will be satisfied.

What are the most common mistakes that occur in productions of your work?
Mistakes are inevitably bound to occur in any production of a play. I don't think I have noted any serious offenses outside of paraphrasing in my work, which in a larger sense can affect how the audience receives some vital information about the characters and the way the story is progressing. It is of the utmost importance to take your time to learn the words and learn their relevance to the story. There is nothing more distracting when watching a play than the actors not understanding the sentence they are saying.

What inspired you to become a playwright?
I have always been a storyteller, but I used to flex that muscle in many different mediums. I spent a lot of time working as an actor, stage manager, costume designer, and director before

even exploring the option of playwriting. I had even originally thought of going into the world of screenwriting, but now I love the world of theatre more than I love the world of cinema and I hope to enrich this world with new stories through this medium. I would have never become a playwright without the mentorship of wonderful people: Keith Salter, who gave me the essential first chance to put up a play of my own and continues to be a wonderful support and champion to this day; Jonathan Dorf, who has been patient in helping me increase my capability and skills as a writer and has served as the ultimate guide and example of what being a professional playwright looks like; Stephen Hancock, another champion whose sharp wit and critical eye has been so beneficial to my growth; and Dee Covington, whose friendship and passion for writing has changed the way I view my life and has helped me understand the invaluable skill of reading your own work critically. The acts of kindness, words of encouragement, and the example of these people's successes not only served as the inspiration that made me want to be a playwright, but still to this day inspires me to continue my work as a playwright.

How did you research the subject?

Instead of doing research, I took a lot from my own experiences and used my imagination to construct the world of the play. The world these characters live in is a heightened version of our own and it's important to remember that it is not realism.

Are any characters modeled after real life or historical figures?

While I was doing the bulk of the writing on this project, I was heavily saturated in the world of babysitting. The girls I was looking after during the summer I wrote this play are two of the liveliest girls I've ever met, and getting to know them was very inspirational to me. I feel that without meeting them, Kitty, as a character, would have never come to life.

Shakespeare gave advice to the players in *Hamlet*; if you could give advice to your cast what would it be?
My primary advice is to have fun. This play isn't heavy or difficult emotionally, but you should still bring yourself to the table. As actors, you can let experiences from your own life inform the performance you give. I encourage open discussion of whether you think the actions of the characters are justified and if you think they are right or wrong for the course of action they took. Theatre makes us more active participants and critical observers of our own lives. Every play you do is an opportunity to experience something new and live out actions you may never otherwise have the chance to live out.

About the Author

Keegon Schuett is a playwright, actor, and director who is currently living and working in Memphis (TN). He studies theatre at the University of Memphis, where he is pursuing a BFA in Theatre Design and Technology and works as a freelance photographer. He discovered a passion for storytelling at a very young age while growing up in the suburbs outside of Philadelphia. He later cultivated an interest in theatre and began performing. He has appeared in over 20 productions, in addition to directing and writing several shows. He has worked in theatre for over 10 years and is very grateful for the support of his family, friends, and mentors that have helped him through creative roadblocks over the years so far.

About YouthPLAYS

YouthPLAYS (www.youthplays.com) is a publisher of award-winning professional dramatists and talented new discoveries, each with an original theatrical voice, and all dedicated to expanding the vocabulary of theatre for young actors and audiences. On our website you'll find one-act and full-length plays and musicals for teen and pre-teen (and even college) actors, as well as duets and monologues for competition. Many of our authors' works have been widely produced at high schools and middle schools, youth theatres and other TYA companies, both amateur and professional, as well as at elementary schools, camps, churches and other institutions serving young audiences and/or actors worldwide. Most are intended for performance by young people, while some are intended for adult actors performing for young audiences.

YouthPLAYS was co-founded by professional playwrights Jonathan Dorf and Ed Shockley. It began merely as an additional outlet to market their own works, which included a substantial body of award-winning published and unpublished plays and musicals. Those interested in their published plays were directed to the respective publishers' websites, and unpublished plays were made available in electronic form. But when they saw the desperate need for material for young actors and audiences—coupled with their experience that numerous quality plays for young people weren't finding a home—they made the decision to represent the work of other playwrights as well. Dozens and dozens of authors are now members of the YouthPLAYS family, with scripts available both electronically and in traditional acting editions. We continue to grow as we look for exciting and challenging plays and musicals for young actors and audiences.

About ProduceaPlay.com

Let's put up a play! Great idea! But producing a play takes time, energy and knowledge. While finding the necessary time and energy is up to you, ProduceaPlay.com is a website designed to assist you with that third element: knowledge.

Created by YouthPLAYS' co-founders, Jonathan Dorf and Ed Shockley, ProduceaPlay.com serves as a resource for producers at all levels as it addresses the many facets of production. As Dorf and Shockley speak from their years of experience (as playwrights, producers, directors and more), they are joined by a group of award-winning theatre professionals and experienced teachers from the world of academic theatre, all making their expertise available for free in the hope of helping this and future generations of producers, whether it's at the school or university level, or in community or professional theatres.

The site is organized into a series of major topics, each of which has its own page that delves into the subject in detail, offering suggestions and links for further information. For example, Publicity covers everything from Publicizing Auditions to How to Use Social Media to Posters to whether it's worth hiring a publicist. Casting details Where to Find the Actors, How to Evaluate a Resume, Callbacks and even Dealing with Problem Actors. You'll find guidance on your Production Timeline, The Theater Space, Picking a Play, Budget, Contracts, Rehearsing the Play, The Program, House Management, Backstage, and many other important subjects.

The site is constantly under construction, so visit often for the latest insights on play producing, and let it help make your play production dreams a reality.

More from YouthPLAYS

Slow by Keegon Schuett
Drama. 45-55 minutes. 1 male, 3 females, 1 either.

Lizzy Slominski is better known to her classmates as "Camera Girl," because she's always hiding behind her digital camera snapping photos of strangers. Her days as a loner end when a mysterious new boy appears at the bus stop. Will she be able to put down her camera and connect, or is she doomed to a life of observing through the lens?

Lockdown by Julia Edwards
Dramedy. 75-90 minutes. 4-6 males, 9-11 females (15 performers total).

It's just another day in the CliffsNotes Library until a siren sounds, the doors lock, and the not-so-studious students discover they are trapped. Did the high-tech security system malfunction again? Is this a sinister state-sanctioned experiment? Then someone hears a gunshot (he thinks), a freaked out substitute teacher is found barricaded in the bathroom, and Crazy Lily has a diabetic seizure. In a claustrophobic pressure-cooker of fear, paranoia, and social strife, this motley crew of hackers, delinquents, surfer dudes, and prom queens must rise above the chaos to save a life and discover the meaning of tolerance along the way.

Of Love and Shampoo by Jonathan Josephson
Comedy. 30-35 minutes. 2 males, 2 females.

Life is pretty awful when you've accidentally locked yourself in the bathroom, especially on the night you're supposed to meet your girlfriend's parents. A madcap comedy about four friends, one very important date, and the locked door that brings them together.

The Locker Next 2 Mine by Jonathan Dorf
Dramedy. 80-85 minutes. 5-12+ males, 8-16+ females (14-40 performers possible).

Alisa arrives at a new high school in the middle of the year to find her locker next to a shrine for a popular lacrosse player who's died in an auto accident, but as she digs deeper, she discovers another death that no one talks about, even as it's left many of the school's students trying to pick up their own pieces. A play about teen suicide and dealing with loss.

The Old New Kid by Adam J. Goldberg
Comedy. 30-40 minutes. 2-9+ males, 3-10+ females (8-30+ performers possible).

It's the half-day of school before Thanksgiving break, and current "new kid" Alan Socrates Bama just wants to get through the day. But when a new-new kid arrives, things change. Alan has three hours to find the meaning of Thanksgiving, survive elementary school politics, battle for his identity, and spell the word "cornucopia" in this *Peanuts*-flavored comedy for kids of all ages.

Camp Monster by Sharyn Rothstein (book and lyrics) and Kris Kukul (music)
Musical. 60-75 minutes. 7-11 males, 8-11 females (15-22 performers possible).

For years, the sons and daughters of the world's most famous monsters (Dracula, The Wicked Witch, Wolfman, and more) have spent their summer at Camp Flonster, the only camp in the world where young monsters can be themselves. But this year, Camp Flonster has a new director, the oppressive and diabolical Roseanne Finicula, who harbors a secret desire to rid the world of all monsters! When the young monsters learn of Roseanne's plot, they must put aside their daily squabbles to work together and beat Roseanne at her own game—and keep the world safe for even the strangest among us.

Made in the USA
San Bernardino, CA
21 September 2015